The Musical Alphabet on the Keys

Written and Designed by Elaine Lombardi

MEL BOOKS
Laguna Woods, California

ISBN 9780986128769
FIRST EDITION, 2018

Library of Congress Cataloging-in-Publication Data
Lombardi, Elaine
The Musical Alphabet on the Keys
written and designed by Elaine Lombardi

Summary: A story using character mnemonics to teach the musical alphabet
on the piano keyboard. Includes sheet music, teaching ideas and printable pages.

ISBN-10: 0986128767
ISBN-13: 978-0-9861287-6-9 (Softcover)

1.   Piano   2. Keyboard   3. Musical Alphabet
I. Lombardi, Elaine   II. Title

Printed in the United States of America

The dog sits in his doghouse
between the two black keys.

G STREET

Grandma's house
on G Street
next to the apple tree.

G

With birdie in his nest singing
" A, B, C, D, E, F, G. "

That's the
musical alphabet
on the keys.

Start with **C** for Cat

and D for Dog

and E for chicken's Egg.

F for Frogs in Grandma's backyard

G for Grandma's Street.

A for Apple

B for Birdie

singing in the tree...

That's the
musical alphabet
on the keys.

The Musical Alphabet on the Keys

Music and Lyrics by Elaine Lombardi

Lyrics:

The dog sits in his dog house be - tween the two black keys.

Grandma's house on G street next to the ap-ple tree. With bird-ie in his

nest sing ing A B C D E F G_ That's the mus-i-cal al-pha-bet on

the keys. Start with C for cat and D for dog and E for chick en's

23 egg— | F for frogs in | Grand-ma's back-yard | G for Grand ma's | street—

28 A for ap-ple | B for bird-ie | sing-ing in the | tree— | That's the | mus-i-cal

34 al-pha-bet | on | the | keys.

Encourage students who do not yet read music to follow along by finding and playing all the musical alphabet keys mentioned in the song. You can also play a pointing or matching game with character music notes included in this book.

C D E F G A B

C D E F G A B

C D E F G A B

C D E F G A B

C D E F G A B

Print, laminate, cut in strips. Place upright behind the piano keys.

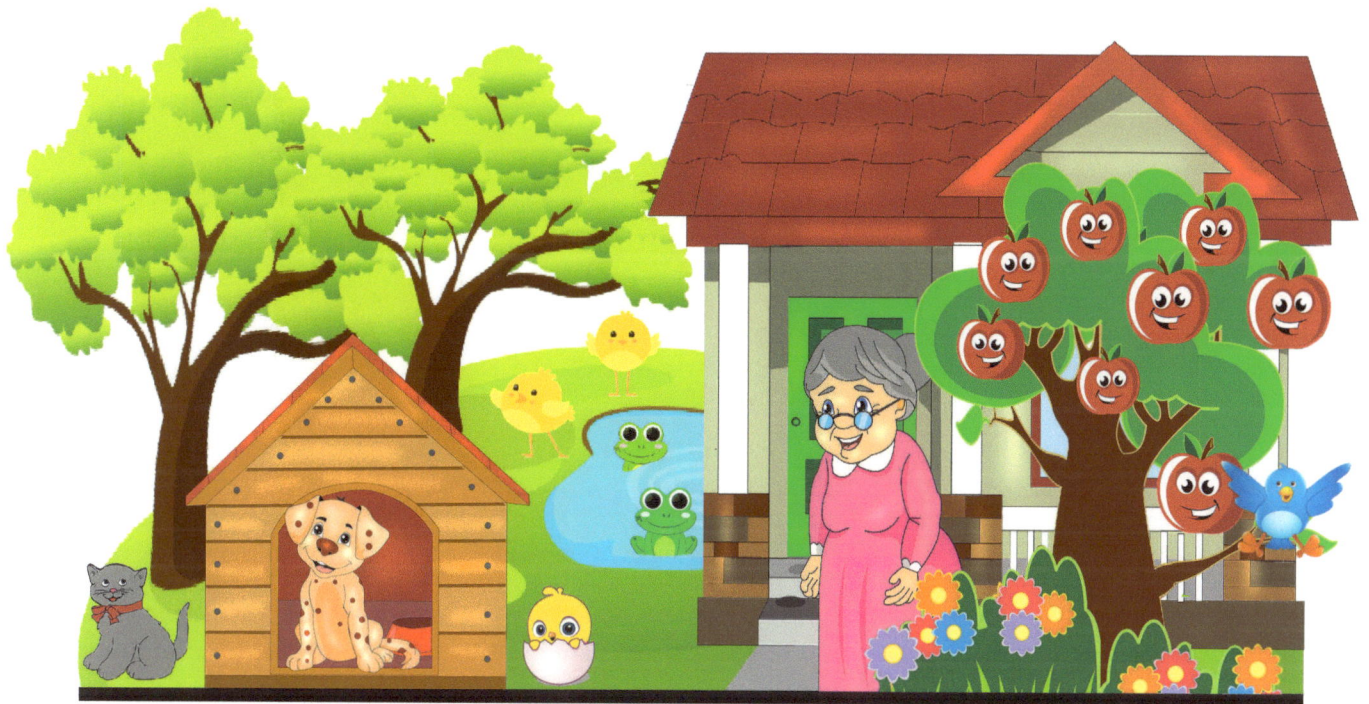

Print the storyboard on heavy card stock. Laminate for extra stability. Cut to stand upright behind the piano keys. The placement of the dog house is behind the two black keys. The characters are designed to line-up properly with each key.

One of the first things I point out to my students is the pattern of two black keys and three black keys found throughout the keyboard. You can talk about the dog walking up the D key to enter his doghouse. Have students find and play all the D keys throughout the keyboard to grasp the repeating patterns.

Likewise, Grandma walks up the G key to her house. Talk about the Apple tree being in front of Grandma's house, and the Frog pond located in the backyard. Mention that she raises chicken's that hatch from Eggs. Add your own twist to the story as you teach your students The Musical Alphabet on the Keys.

Copy and print the following pages to play any matching games.

A B C D
E F G # *b*

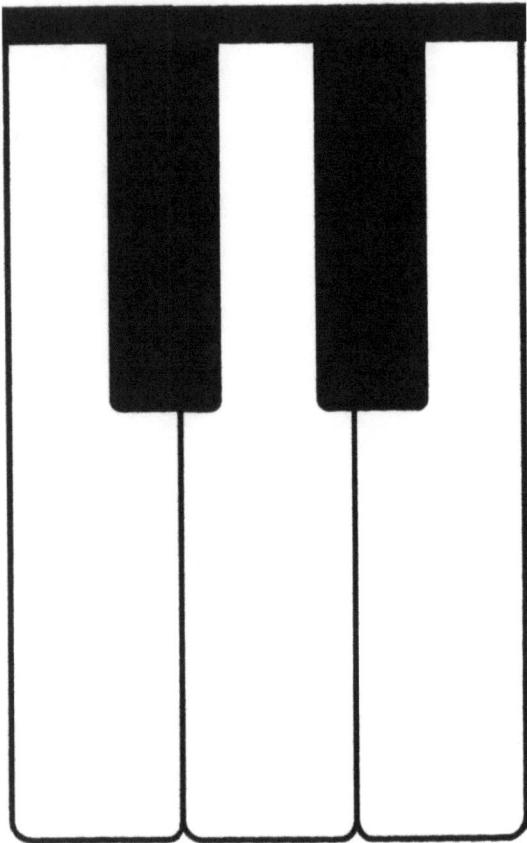

Print, laminate and cut out several copies to make a keyboard puzzle.

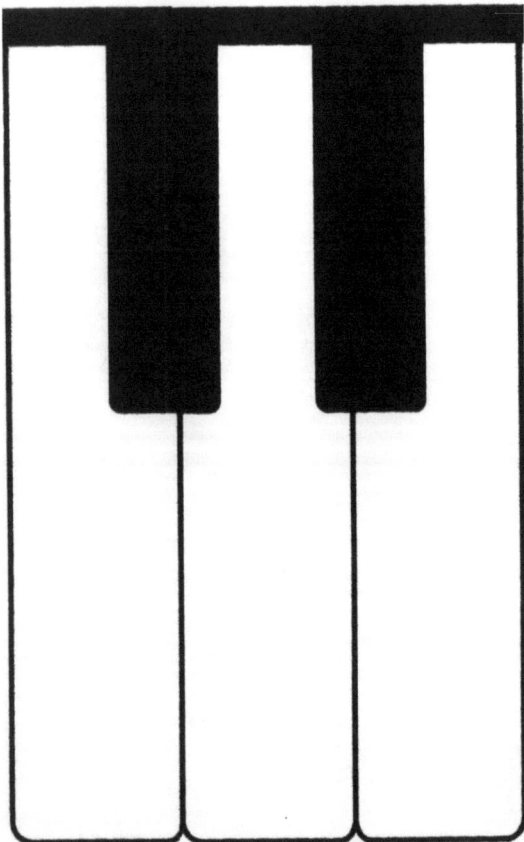

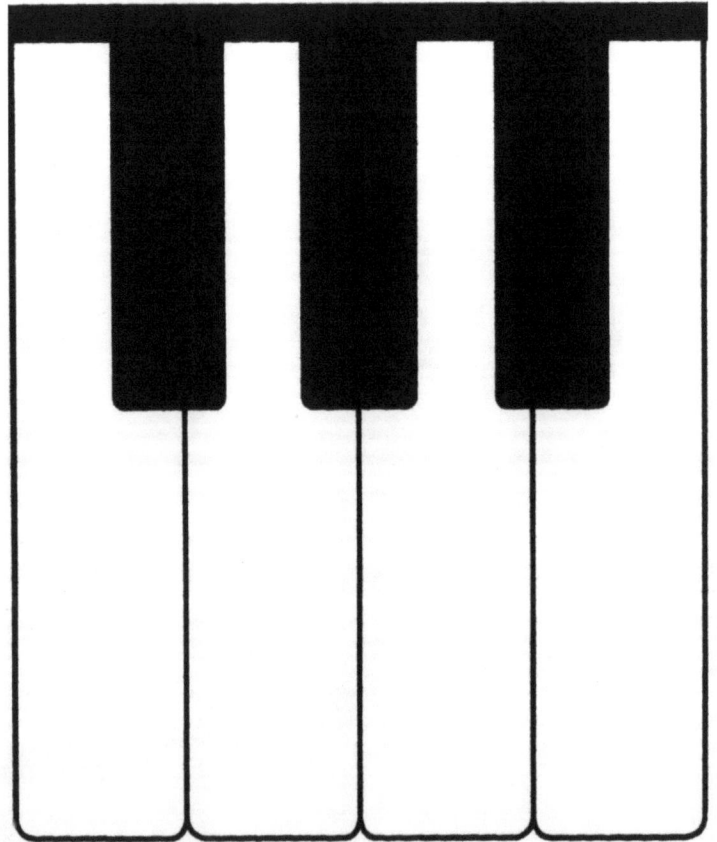

About the Author

Miss Elaine's ability to keep her students engaged during their piano lessons comes from her belief that we learn best when we are having fun. Knowing how children learn through play is the principle she has built her career on.

Visit her website at VillagePianoLessons.com

www.ingramcontent.com/pod-product-compliance
Lightning Source LLC
Chambersburg PA
CBHW041224040426
42443CB00002B/77